A New True Book

INTERNET

By Lora Koehler

CHILDREN'S PRESS
A Division of Grolier Publishing
Sherman Turnpike
Danbury, Connecticut 06816

You can use e-mail on the Internet
to keep in touch with friends.

PHOTO CREDITS

Monty McAdoo–screen captures: 32 (right), 36

© Cameramann International, Ltd.–9 (left), 16 (left)

FPG International–© Micheal Simpson, 13

© Fred Hayes–2, 15 (right), 20, 32 (left), 45

Lora Koehler–screen capture: 28

MGA/Photri–© Mark E. Gibson, 7 (inset)

NASA–24

PhotoEdit–© David Young-Wolff, 4, 15 (left), 23; © Tony Freeman, 7 (right), 16 (right), 17, 33 (left); © Tom McCarthy, 18 (right); © Paul Conklin, 26

Photri–© Jack Novak, 33 (right)

Tom Stack & Associates–© TSADO, 11

Tony Stone Images–8; © Chip Henderson, Cover; © Robert E. Daemmrich, 18 (left), 31; © Arthur Tilley, 35

Unicorn Stock Photos–© Aneal Vohra, 7; © MacDonald Photography, 43

UPI/Bettmann Newsphotos–screen captures: 30, 37, 39

COVER: Boy working on computer in library

Project Editor: Fran Dyra
Design: Margrit Fiddle
Photo Research: Feldman & Associates, Inc.

Library of Congress Cataloging-in-Publication Data

Koehler, Lora.
    Internet / by Lora Koehler.
        p.   cm.–(A New true book)
    Includes index.
    ISBN 0-516-01079-4
    1. Internet (Computer network)–Juvenile literature.
[1. Internet (Computer network)] I. Title. II. Series.
TK5105.875.I57K64 1995   94-38069
004.6'7–dc20   CIP
                                                          AC

With love to Fred and thanks to Chris Tomer and Bernard Asbell, for the motivation and encouragement they've provided

TABLE OF CONTENTS

WHAT IS THE INTERNET?

Suppose you could sit down at a computer, type in a few commands, and get a new computer game–or read messages from a friend in Oregon about the latest Marvel comics series. Then maybe you'd like to write to your state representative about your thoughts on school and the educational system.

Could you do all this from one computer? You could if your computer was connected to the Internet.

The Internet is a network of computers. When computers are "networked" it means that all the computers in the system are connected.

You could compare the Internet to the highway system in the United States. When you look at a map, you see that all of those highways connect. If

A map of the roads in the United States can help you picture
what the Internet looks like.   Inset: The Golden Gate Bridge

you want to go from your
house to the Golden Gate
Bridge, you could drive there
by many different routes.

To help you imagine
what the Internet is like,

Like people on the highways, information on
the Internet can travel by many routes.

picture the many
connections and routes of
our nation's highways, and
the great speed with which
we travel those highways. It's
easy to see why
people sometimes call the

Internet an "information superhighway." The "roads" that connect the computers are cables and wires— sometimes the same wires that give you telephone service provide access to the Internet.

The huge Internet network

Information is sent through cables and wires.

is made up of smaller networks. In many ways, the structure of these networks mirrors that of the U.S. government. For instance, the Internet has a national network, like our federal government; regional networks, like our state governments; and local networks, like our local governments. Our country's national network connects with the networks of other countries—the Internet stretches worldwide.

WHERE DID IT COME FROM?

While NASA was busy putting men on the moon in 1969, the Department of Defense started ARPANET.

The Internet began in 1969 with only four computers. It was a Department of Defense network known as ARPANET.

Thanks to its military beginnings, Internet users can take many routes to get to the same place. Computers connected by a single wire could be easily disconnected, so the military designed a system with multiple connections between computers. If one route is down, the information is automatically sent by another route.

The president and Congress have proposed the development of a

Only twenty-three computers were connected to the Internet in 1981. Today, there are nearly one million.

National Information Infrastructure (NII) to promote growth of the Internet network. They hope that everyone will someday be able to access such a network.

13

WHAT DO I NEED TO KNOW?

To use the Internet you need to know:

- A postal system on the Internet: E-mail
- Where to meet people: Listservs and Newsgroups
- How to go places: Telnet
- How to move things: FTP
- How to find things: Gopher, Archie, Veronica, WWW, WAIS

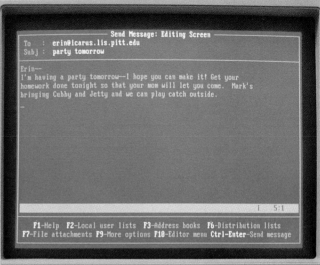

Send Message: Editing Screen
To   : erin@icarus.lis.pitt.edu
Subj : party tomorrow

Erin--
I'm having a party tomorrow--I hope you can make it! Get your
homework done tonight so that your mom will let you come. Mark's
bringing Cubby and Jetty and we can play catch outside.
--

                                                        I   5:1

F1-Help F2-Local user lists F3-Address books F6-Distribution lists
F7-File attachments F9-More options F10-Editor menu Ctrl-Enter-Send message

A house has an address so that mail can be delivered. If you want to receive mail on the Internet you need an Internet address, like the one shown in the "To" line of this e-mail message.

A POSTAL SYSTEM: E-MAIL

E-mail allows you to send and receive messages in much the same way as the post office does. Of course the post office delivers mail to your house address, while e-mail delivers messages

When sent the traditional way, a message can take days to arrive at its destination.

to your Internet address.

The difference is in the time it takes. To use the postal system you have to write the letter, put it in an envelope, address and stamp the envelope, and mail it. Then it might take a week before it's delivered! That's why

Internet users call the postal system "snail mail."

With e-mail, you type your message with an address at the top and press a few keys to send it. The message will probably reach its destination in less time than it takes to sing "Take Me Out to the Ballgame."

On the Internet, your message can be there in minutes.

Whether your interest is baseball or ballet, you can probably find a listserv that suits.

WHERE TO MEET PEOPLE: LISTSERVS AND NEWSGROUPS

You probably know at least a few people who

like to talk about the same things you do. Friends who collect baseball cards, or a neighbor who enjoys ballet. Sometimes they tell you interesting things that you didn't already know, and sometimes you share things with them.

The Internet has many groups of people who share such interests. The people in a specific group might live in different countries, but their thoughts can travel far and

You can learn a lot from the information people share on a listserv.

move fast through electronic messages. The groups may be called listservs, discussion groups, bulletin boards, or newsgroups, but they all serve the same basic purpose—getting groups of people together to "talk" about the things they like.

The people don't actually talk, of course. They send messages to a central place where everyone can read them. Or, the messages are sent back out to people who "subscribe" to the group's list (like you subscribe to a magazine).

HOW TO GO PLACES: TELNET

Using telnet can take you places—from the computer you're sitting in front of to another computer. That other computer could be in the next room—or clear across the country.

Either way, it's worth the trip.

For example, suppose you heard on the radio that you'll be able to see

the space shuttle on the
horizon at sunset, and
you're curious about its
payload. You telnet to
NASA's database, where
you find out that the

Space shuttle payloads are just one of the
things you could research using telnet.

shuttle is carrying experiments designed by science students just like you.

There are many databases like NASA's on the Internet. You can use them to find information, just as you would use an encyclopedia or an almanac. Like books, different databases offer different information. For example, you could search one of these databases to find the latitude and longitude of Pittsburgh. Or you could telnet to a library catalog to see if that library has the book you want.

With telnet you don't have to go to the library to browse for books.

HOW TO MOVE THINGS: FTP

Sometimes you may want to move things over the Internet. Maybe you want to give a friend a computer program, or retrieve the tale of *Frankenstein* from a service called Project Gutenberg.

You can do this by using FTP (*File Transfer Protocol*). A protocol is a set of rules.

Many FTP sites contain

```
icarus.lis[3] % ftp
ftp> help
Commands may be abbreviated.   Commands are:

!                cr               macdef           proxy            send
$                delete           mdelete          sendport         status
account          debug            mdir             put              struct
append           dir              mget             pwd              sunique
ascii            disconnect       mkdir            quit             tenex
bell             form             mls              quote            trace
binary           get              mode             recv             type
bye              glob             mput             remotehelp       user
case             hash             nmap             rename           verbose
cd               help             ntrans           reset            ?
cdup             lcd              open             rmdir
close            ls               prompt           runique
ftp>
```

Typing "help" at the FTP prompt gives you a list of commands.
You can get more information on a command by typing
"help" followed by the command, such as "help cd."

files that anyone can copy.
Using these FTP sites is
known as "anonymous
FTP" because you type in
"anonymous" (meaning
"unknown") when asked for
your log-on.

HOW TO FIND THINGS: GOPHER, ARCHIE, VERONICA, WWW, WAIS

When you're using e-mail, telnet, or FTP, you might sometimes feel that you're stumbling along in the dark with no idea where to find what you need. Perhaps a flashlight would help. Gopher, Archie, Veronica, WWW (*World-Wide Web*), and

WAIS (*Wide Area Information Server*) are all flashlights of a sort; they are Internet tools that can help you find your way to the information you need. Gopher is menu-driven. You select where you want

Hundreds of institutions worldwide have accessible Gopher servers. You can find information on any of the Gopher menus at these institutions.

```
Internet Gopher Information Client 2.0 pl8

            Other Gopher and Information Servers

 -->  1.  All the Gopher Servers in the World/
      2.  Search All the Gopher Servers in the World <?>
      3.  Search titles in Gopherspace using veronica/
      4.  Africa/
      5.  Asia/
      6.  Europe/
      7.  International Organizations/
      8.  Middle East/
      9.  North America/
     10.  Pacific/
     11.  Russia/
     12.  South America/
     13.  Terminal Based Information/
     14.  WAIS Based Information/
     15.  Gopher Server Registration. <??>












Press ? for Help, q to Quit, u to go up a menu          Page: 1/1
  1:20    24x80    2k    19200 N81
```

Tools like Gopher and Archie can help you find the information you need.

to go or what you want to view from a number of choices listed on your screen.

Archie is a command-driven search tool. Using Archie is a little like knowing the password to

```
                    Source Selection                    Sources: 541

   #            Server              Source                   Cost
523:   [wais.house.gov]         USHOUSE_congress_info         Free
524:   [wais.house.gov]         USHOUSE_GATT_treaty           Free
525:   [wais.house.gov]         USHOUSE_house_bill_text_103rd Free
526:   [wais.house.gov]         USHOUSE_house_bill_text_104th Free
527:   [oac.hsc.uth.tmc.edu]    ut-research-expertise         Free
528:   [borg.lib.vt.edu]        vpiej-1                       Free
529:   [wais.wu-wien.ac.at]     wafe                          Free
530:   [server.wais.com]        wais-discussion-archives      Free
531:   [quake.think.com]        wais-docs                     Free
532:   [server.wais.com]        wais-talk-archives            Free
533:   [hermes.ecn.purdue.ed]   water-quality                 Free
534:   [quake.think.com]        weather                       Free
535:   [sunsite.unc.edu]        Welsh                         Free
536:   [163.231.231.3]          Wests-Legal-Directory         Free
537:   [sunsite.unc.edu]        White-House-Papers            Free
538:   [cmns-moon.think.com]    world-factbook                Free
539:   [gopher.uwo.ca]          world-factbook93              Free
540:   [wais.wu-wien.ac.at]     wu-wien-phonebk               Free

Keywords:

<space> selects, w for keywords, arrows move, <return> searches,
q quits, or ?
```

Some databases specialize in certain types of information (for instance, environmental). With WAIS, you can select the databases that you think are more likely to contain the information you want. The screen shown on the right is an example of a WAIS source selection screen.

open a door–if you say "open sesame," the door opens and you go in. Likewise, when you type the correct commands, Archie conducts your search. With WAIS, you use both commands and menus.

Using Veronica is a little like using the online catalog at the library.

Using Veronica is like searching the online catalog at the library. And with WWW, you don't have to type at all; you just point your mouse and click.

33

Of these Internet tools, Gopher, Veronica, and WWW are especially easy for the beginner to use.

-Gopher-

Gopher was developed at the University of Minnesota. The researchers wanted to design a program that would enable students and teachers to find things on the Internet. Above all, they wanted it to be easy to use.

To help you understand
how Gopher works, picture
a rodent burrowing through
tunnels and into nests to
find things. When you use
Gopher, you burrow
through the system by
choosing items from a

```
        University of Minnesota Gopher
--> 1.   Information About Gopher/
    2.   Computer Information/
    3.   Discussion Groups/
    4.   Fun & Games/
    5.   Internet file server (ftp) sites/
    6.   Libraries/
    7.   News/
    8.   Other Gopher and Information Servers/
    9.   Phone Books/
   10.   Search Gopher Titles at the University of Minnesota <?>
   11.   Search lots of places at the University of Minnesota <?>
   12.   University of Minnesota Campus Information/



   Press ? for Help, q to Quit, u to go up a menu
   Page: 1/1
```

The opening Gopher screen at the University of Minnesota, where the Gopher program was developed.

menu. You can go backward by choosing the menu item that you just came from. Or you can tunnel forward by choosing another item from the menu.

Even though Gopher was

```
Press ? for Help, q to Quit, u to go up a menu       Retrieving Directory..|
                     Internet Gopher Information Client 2.0 p18

                            AskERIC InfoGuides

  --█  1.  New - Fall 1994 AskERIC Infoguides/
       2.  AskERIC InfoGuides on Library Technology (12/2/94)/
       3.  Search AskERIC InfoGuides <?>
       4.  AIDS Education.
       5.  African History - 1.
       6.  African History - 2.
       7.  American History.
       8.  Anthropology.
       9.  Arts Therapy.
      10.  Astronomy.
      11.  Authentic Assessment.
      12.  Business Information.
      13.  Business and Economics.
      14.  Central and South American Indians.
      15.  Chemistry .
      16.  Chemistry for Kids.
      17.  Child Abuse.
      18.  Children's Literature.

Press █ for Help, █ to Quit, █ to go up a menu                  Page: 1/4
```

An example of the Gopher menu. You can move forward to another menu or item by moving the cursor to the number with the arrow keys and pressing return. To go up to a previous menu press u, as the commands at the bottom of the screen show.

designed to find things, it works better if you have some idea where the information you want might be located. If you have no idea at all, you might be better off using Veronica.

-Veronica-

You can use Veronica to find things the same way you would use an online catalog at the library. For instance, you want information on cats, so you type *CATS.* If you use the library's catalog, it lists books that deal with cats. If you use Veronica, you get a list of databases that have information on this subject.

Internet Gopher Information Client 2.0 p10

Find GOPHER DIRECTORIES by Title word(s) (via University of Pisa): cat

```
-->  1.  9407001_Cat States and Single Runs for the Damped Harmonic Oscilla../
     2.  9402005_CHIRAL SYMMETRY, RENORMALIZATION GROUP AND FIXED POINTS FO../
     3.  9210220_The Cheshire Cat Bag Model: Color Anomaly and $\eta'$ Prop../
     4.  9310300_CHESHIRE CAT HADRONS" By Mannque Rho (SPhT..lata, Argentina)/
     5.  9312106_Even and odd coherent states (Schroedinger cat states) for../
     6.  Persian Cat/
     7.  Siamese Cat/
     8.  9307005_On the Quantum Cat and Sawtooth Maps- Return to Generic Be../
     9.  rpoA-cat/
    10.  sigB-cat/
    11.  rpoA-cat/
    12.  sigB-cat/
    13.  Cat-301 Proteoglycan (Cat-301)/
    14.  Cat-301 Proteoglycan (CAT-301)/
    15.  cat/
    16.  cat/
```

The results of a Veronica search for the word CAT.
Numbers 6 and 7 look like items to pursue further.

Veronica put this list
together by looking at all
the Gopher menus
mentioned in the previous
section for the word *CATS.*
When you select an item

39

from the list Veronica has provided, Veronica takes you to that Gopher server and you can look at the information.

As easy as Veronica is to use, the next search tool–WWW–is even easier.

-*WWW*-

WWW–or "the Web"–is designed so that you can use a technology called hypertext to browse for information on the Internet.
Using hypertext, you can

```
Beethoven            Sym. 5, 6
Mozart               Piano concerto 21, 23
Chopin               Piano concerto 1, 2
Beethoven            Piano concerto 5
Beethoven            Piano c. 3
Dvorak               Cello concerto
Tchaikovsky          Variations
Beethoven            Sym. 9
Beethoven            Sym. 7, 8
Tchaikovsky          Violin concertos
Schubert, Beethoven  Streichquartette
Tchaikovsky          Sym. 1
Yale Cellos          Sound of
Tchaikovsky          Sym. 6
Strauss              Alpen
Beethoven            Sonate
Tchaikovsky          Piano concerto 1
                     Sym. 4
Blues Trottoir       Histoires Courtes
Vollenweider         Book Of Roses
-- press space for next page --
  Arrow keys: Up and Down to move. Right to follow a link; Left to go back.
  H)elp O)ptions P)rint G)o M)ain screen Q)uit /=search [delete]=history list
```

This screen shows part of a Web document. Directions for following hypertext "links" (the underlined words) are shown at the bottom of the screen.

"jump" from one place to another by selecting certain words. The words you can select are highlighted, or may be followed by numbers in parentheses. The

41

documents you can jump between are "linked."

Say, for instance, that you're reading a text about Beethoven that you found on the Web. You see *violin,* so you select it and automatically jump to another article about violins. When you've read that one, you might want to go back to the original article on Beethoven. Or perhaps you've found another link you want to follow.

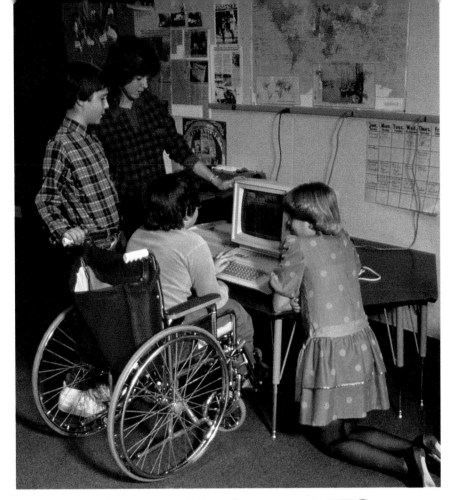

WHAT'S NEXT?

Now you know what the Internet is. To start using the Internet, you need to know certain commands and procedures. Good

sources of information include "how to" guides to the Internet and the help screens you'll find when you use Internet tools. In addition, your school or library might provide help sheets.

As you begin exploring, keep in mind that things don't always work the way they're supposed to. If you can't find what you want, perhaps you've made a mistake. But you might simply need to try again

Whether you're in Malaysia or Massachusetts, a connection to the Internet puts you in touch with a world of information and people.

later, or try a different resource.

So don't be overwhelmed by the amount of information... what you need is out there, somewhere. Internet will help you find what you want.

WORDS YOU SHOULD KNOW

Archie (AR • chee)–a command-driven information search tool

command (kuh • MAND)–a word, phrase, or character string that is typed in to tell the computer what to do

computer network (kum • PYOO • ter NET • werk)–a group of computers connected by cables or wires

database (DAY • ta • baiss)–a collection of information. An electronic database is stored on a computer

e-mail (EE • mayl)–a way of sending electronic messages. Also used to refer to the electronic messages themselves

FTP (*File Transfer Protocol*) (FYLE TRANZ • fer PRO • tuh• kawl)– allows you to transfer information over the Internet

Gopher (GO • fer)–a menu-driven information search tool

hypertext link (HY • per • text LINK)–a connection established between documents

Internet (IN • ter • net)–a worldwide network of computers

listservs, discussion groups, bulletin boards, newsgroups (LIHST • servz, dis • KUSH • un GROOPS, BULL • ih • tin BORDZ, NOOZ • groops)–services that allow people who share common interests to exchange information

menu (MEN • yoo)–a list of options

Project Gutenberg (PRAH • jekt GOO • tin • berg)–a database that contains the full texts of books like *Alice in Wonderland* and *Frankenstein*

protocol (PRO • tuh • kawl)–a set of rules

telnet (TEL • net)–a protocol that enables you to log-on to a computer other than the one you are physically using

Veronica (vuh • RON • ik • ah)—a search tool used to find information on gopher servers. To use it, you type in the word or words you are looking for

WAIS (*Wide Area Information Server*)
(WYD AIR • ee • ya in • fer • MAY • shun SER • ver)—a search tool that retrieves information based on the words you type in and the sources you select

WWW (*World Wide Web*) (WORLD WYDE WEB)—a hypertext-based tool used to browse for information on the Internet

INDEX

About the Author

Lora Koehler received her own introduction to the Internet while obtaining a master's degree in library science. She has worked in writing, editing, and public relations. Ms. Koehler is a member of the American Library Association and the Association for Library Service to Children. In addition to technology, her interests include hiking and the outdoors.